PHOTOSHOP FOR BEGINNERS (BOOK 3)

A step-by-step guide to understanding image basics in Photoshop

Brian Indigo

Table of Content

Choosing the appropriate file format for web, print, and other mediums

Balancing file size and image quality

Saving and exporting images in different formats in Photoshop

Conclusion

Introduction

Welcome to the world of Photoshop, the industry standard for editing and manipulating images. This tutorial is intended to help you learn how to use Photoshop's amazing potential, whether you're a novice or someone trying to improve your abilities.

Images are very important in our lives today, from amateur photography to business graphic design. This is especially true in the digital era. With its extensive collection of tools and capabilities that enable users to realize their creative ambitions, Photoshop has grown to be regarded as the industry standard for image manipulation.

Photoshop gives you the ability to convert commonplace photographs into spectacular works of art. There are many options, from picture editing and enhancement to amazing compositions and digital artwork.

You'll go through Photoshop's foundational ideas with the help of this manual. We will examine key tools and methods, gain knowledge of picture fundamentals like resolution and color modes, and dig into more sophisticated features like layers, filters, and text manipulation.

Understanding Photoshop may significantly help you achieve your objectives, whether you want to become a professional graphic designer or just want to improve your social media presence. To help you use this incredible program to its greatest capacity, this book will provide detailed instructions, useful advice, and creative inspiration.

So, get your creative juices flowing and start this Photoshop journey. Discover the amazing things Photoshop can produce as we explore the realm of digital images.

What are images and their significance in digital design?

Images are depictions of things, situations, or ideas that have been photographed, digitally created, or graphically designed. Images are essential to the communication of ideas, arousal of feelings, and improvement of a design's overall visual appeal in the context of digital design.

The following points may be used to describe the importance of pictures in digital design:

❖ **Visual communication:** Images are effective instruments for conveying concepts and knowledge. In a manner that words alone cannot, they may quickly communicate a message or tell a narrative.

- ❖ **Emotional Impact:** Imagery has the power to elicit feelings and establish a connection with the observer. The appropriate visuals may provoke certain emotional reactions and help designers engage their audience more deeply.

- ❖ **Branding and Identity:** Images are essential for building a brand's identity and producing an enduring visual impression. Brand distinction and identification are aided by logos, symbols, and other visual components.

- ❖ **Aesthetic Appeal:** Images offer visual interest and improve the overall aesthetics of a design, which increases its aesthetic appeal. They may be employed to provide harmony, balance, and focus points, which will enhance the design's aesthetic attractiveness and keep the viewer's attention.

❖ **User Experience:** Images are essential in the user interface (UI) and user experience (UX) design because they help people navigate, provide visual clues, and enhance the usability of a digital product or website.

❖ **Storytelling and Narrative:** Images may be utilized to tell tales and communicate narratives in an engrossing and absorbing manner. They may draw viewers in, evoke a mood, and bring ideas to life.

How do images relate to Photoshop and its capabilities?

Since Photoshop is an advanced program made especially for editing and manipulating images, images are at the heart of its capabilities. For photographers, graphic designers, and digital artists, Photoshop is a crucial tool because it offers a variety of tools and functions that allow users to deal with pictures in a variety of ways.

Users of Photoshop have access to a wide range of picture editing options, including but not limited to:

* **Editing:** Users may modify brightness, contrast, color balance, and other picture qualities using Photoshop's robust editing features. Additionally, users may repair flaws, eliminate undesired features, and improve picture details.

❖ **Image manipulation:** is made simple using Photoshop by the user's ability to effortlessly resize, crop, rotate, and modify pictures. Users may make compositions, combine several photographs, or remove certain things thanks to the software's exact control over image components.

❖ **Repair and restoration:** options are available in Photoshop for old or damaged photos. More senior photos may be given new life by users by removing scratches, stains, and other flaws.

❖ **Effects and Filters:** Photoshop has a large selection of artistic effects and filters that enable users to add artistic touches, replicate different textures and styles, and improve the visual impact of their photographs.

- ❖ **Text and Graphics:** Users may use Photoshop to easily include text and graphics in their photographs. Typography, logo design, and the addition of other visual components to photos are all made possible by the program.

- ❖ **Workflow and Automation:** Photoshop contains tools such as layers, masks, and adjustment tools that automate the picture editing process. Users may also automate monotonous operations using actions and scripts to increase productivity and save time.

In conclusion, Photoshop and photos go hand in hand. Users may edit, modify, recover, improve, and change photographs using Photoshop's tools in a precise and imaginative manner.

Chapter 1

Image Resolution and Size

How significant is image resolution, and what is it?

Image resolution, expressed in terms of pixels per inch (PPI) or dots per inch (DPI), is the degree of clarity and detail in a picture. It directly affects an image's clarity and sharpness by deciding how many pixels it contains.

The influence of picture resolution on an image's ultimate output is what gives it its significance. More pixels mean finer details, softer edges, and greater visual quality overall in a picture with a higher resolution. As lower-resolution photos could seem pixelated or unclear when printed or viewed on high-resolution displays, this is especially important when dealing with images that will be used in such contexts.

The capacity to edit and resize photos without suffering a major loss in quality is also impacted by image resolution. Higher-quality photographs provide you with more options for cropping, resizing, and editing, giving you more control and accuracy when manipulating your images.

The size of a picture's file is also influenced by the resolution of the image. Higher-quality photographs often have bigger file sizes, which might affect website loading speeds, upload/download times, and the amount of storage needed.

Whether your photographs are meant for print, the web, or other digital media, it's critical to comprehend and choose the right image resolution in order to satisfy the precise specifications of your intended output. By selecting the appropriate resolution, you may get the best possible picture quality and make sure that your graphics successfully tell the tale or express the message you want them to.

Understanding pixels, DPI, and PPI

The little components that make up a computer image are known as pixels, or "picture elements." A single point of color information is represented by each pixel. An image's resolution and amount of detail increase with the number of pixels present.

The term "dots per inch" (DPI), which stands for "dots per inch," describes how many ink dots a printer can print on one inch of paper. For printed photos, it is most important. A printing that is finer and more detailed often has a higher DPI rating.

PPI stands for "pixels per inch" and describes how many pixels make up an inch of a digital picture. It has to do with the resolution of the picture and how it will seem on digital displays or when printed. A higher PPI number indicates a more detailed, higher-quality picture.

The link between pixels, DPI, and PPI should be taken into account while dealing with digital pictures. For instance, a high-resolution photograph will have a bigger file size and more pixels per inch, which will result in superior quality and clarity when viewed or printed at a smaller scale. However, since there are fewer pixels available per inch when printing or displaying a picture at a greater scale, the image may seem pixelated.

Making educated judgments about image editing, scaling, and output settings requires an understanding of pixels, DPI, and PPI. You can guarantee that your digital photographs will have the required amount of detail and clarity when printed or displayed by tweaking these settings.

Choosing the right resolution for different purposes

When dealing with digital photographs, it is essential to choose the appropriate resolution for various applications. An image's resolution defines how clear and detailed it is, and it has a significant influence on how it will seem and work in different situations. The following suggestions can help you choose the right resolution:

❖ **Online and Digital Displays:** A resolution of 72 pixels per inch (PPI) is often enough for pictures intended for online usage. On displays like those found in computers, tablets, and smartphones, this resolution makes the picture clear and loads fast.

❖ **Print:** The ideal resolution to use when preparing photos for printing depends on the desired quality and the printing process. For high-quality printing, a resolution of 300 PPI is often regarded as normal. However, a lesser resolution of around 150-200 PPI may be appropriate for large-format prints or circumstances where the picture would be seen from a distance.

❖ **Social media:** The picture size requirements for various social media networks vary. To guarantee that your photographs appear appropriately and prevent any quality loss or cropping, it is essential to verify the recommended resolutions for each platform.

- ❖ **Retouching and editing:** It's best to start with a high-resolution photograph when working on intricate retouching or editing jobs. As a result, there is greater flexibility and the ability to make exact modifications without compromising picture quality.

Keep in mind that a low-resolution image's quality won't suddenly improve by raising the resolution. If you expect to require bigger prints or in-depth editing, it is always ideal to start with a high-resolution photograph.

Resizing and resampling images in Photoshop

A vital skill that enables you to modify the proportions and overall size of a picture to suit various needs is the ability to resize and resample images in Photoshop. Powerful tools are available in Photoshop to help you change images, whether you need to make them smaller for online usage or larger for printing. The following steps can help;

❖ **Picture Size:** Choose "Image Size" from the "Image" menu to enlarge a picture. The image's current size and resolution are shown in a dialog box that will pop up. New width, height, and resolution values may be entered here. A good choice for a unit of measurement is one of pixels, inches, or centimeters.

❖ **Resampling Options:** Photoshop has a variety of resampling options to manage the redistribution of pixels while scaling. The two most often used choices are "Bicubic" and "Bilinear." While bilinear interpolation is good for expanding the size of a picture, bicubic interpolation is best for shrinking it. These choices reduce pixelation or loss of detail and help preserve picture quality.

❖ **Aspect Ratio:** Maintaining the image's original aspect ratio while scaling is crucial to preventing distortion. Make sure the "Constrain Proportions" or "Maintain Aspect Ratio" checkbox is checked to do this. In this manner, changing the width or height of one dimension will cause the other to update automatically.

❖ **Preview and Apply Changes:**
Photoshop shows a preview of the final
picture size when you change the
dimensions or resolution. Preview and
Apply Changes. Utilize this chance to
assess the adjustments' aesthetic effect.
To apply the resizing, click "OK" after
you are finished.

P.S: Keep in mind that altering a photograph,
particularly when expanding, might impact its
quality. Although enlargement may cause some
sharpness or detail loss, generally speaking,
decreasing the size preserves greater picture
quality.

Avoiding common pitfalls and maintaining image quality

To preserve ideal picture quality while scaling
and resampling photos in Photoshop, it's crucial

to be aware of frequent hazards. For advice on avoiding these traps, read on:

- ❖ **Keep the Original:** Before making any modifications, it's a good idea to make a backup or copy of the original picture. As a result, if necessary, you may always return to the original version.

- ❖ **Avoid Excessive Enlargement:** Although Photoshop has an enlargement feature, it's crucial to be careful when doing so. Loss of clarity and pixelation may occur when images are enlarged excessively. In order to preserve picture quality, try to keep the enlargement within bounds.

- ❖ **Watch Out for Low Quality:** Before downsizing, make sure the image's quality is sufficient for the purpose for which it will be used. Images with low quality might seem fuzzy or pixelated, especially when printed or viewed at greater sizes. For your chosen media, such as the web or print, aim for a resolution that satisfies its specifications.

* **Using sharpening techniques:** is a good idea since occasionally resizing a picture causes the sharpness to disappear. Applying the proper sharpening procedures may help to improve the image's clarity and details. Use selective sharpening to target certain regions or try out various sharpening filters.

* **Examine and Preview:** To assess the quality of the resized picture, always zoom in or examine it at 100%. Any artifacts, rough edges, or loss of details should be noticed. Before completing the

modifications, make corrections if required.

- ❖ **Choose the Appropriate File Format:** When saving the downsized picture, do it in the format that best serves its needs. Think about JPEG or PNG with optimum settings if you want to utilize them on the web. To preserve picture data and improve printing outcomes, select high-quality formats like TIFF or PSD for printing.

You may keep the quality of your images when resizing and resampling in Photoshop if you are aware of these typical dangers and take the appropriate safeguards. To ensure that your photographs seem professional and aesthetically pleasing in every situation, try to strike the most outstanding possible balance between size and quality.

Chapter 2

Color Modes and Bit Depth

Introduction to color modes (RGB, CMYK, Grayscale)

The representation and display of colors are controlled by color modes, which are crucial components of digital design and picture editing. The three basic color modes in Photoshop that are often used are RGB, CMYK, and Grayscale. Each mode has special qualities and uses. Let's look at them:

❖ **Red, Green, and Blue, or RGB,** is an additive color model used on digital devices and displays. It produces a broad spectrum of colors by combining red, green, and blue light at various intensities. Web design, digital graphics, and screen viewing all benefit greatly from RGB. Colors that are ideal for digital media are rich and lively.

❖ **Cyan, Magenta, Yellow, and Black, or CMYK,** is a subtractive color model that is largely used in printing. It generates colors by taking light away from the white backdrop. For print-related products like brochures, flyers, or posters, CMYK is appropriate. When computer designs are translated to ink on paper, the colors are more faithfully portrayed.

❖ **Grayscale** is a color mode that displays pictures in various tones of gray. It just uses various shades of black and white instead of colors. For creative purposes, some printing tasks, and black-and-white photography when color is not required, grayscale is often employed.

To get the desired visual result, it is essential to comprehend and choose the correct color mode in Photoshop. While CMYK is appropriate for print work, RGB is best for digital designs. When dealing with photographs that are in black and white or when color is not necessary, grayscale is employed.

Knowing the Differences Between and Uses of Each Color Mode

Color modes are important in digital design because they govern how colors are shown and represented. RGB, CMYK, and Grayscale are the three main color options in Photoshop. Each mode has a set of unique qualities and uses. Let's examine them in more depth:

- ❖ **RGB (Red, Green, Blue):** For digital media, RGB is an additive color mode. A broad variety of colors are produced by mixing red, green, and blue at various intensities. For screen-based tasks like digital art, social media graphics, and site design, RGB is the best option. It has a wide color spectrum that is vivid and suitable for digital displays.

- ❖ **Cyan, Magenta, Yellow, and Black, or CMYK**, is a subtractive color mode that is predominantly used in print printing. A whole spectrum of colors is produced using four ink colors: cyan, magenta, yellow, and black. Brochures, flyers, posters, and other marketing materials may all be created in CMYK for printing. For output on paper with ink, it offers precise color representation.

- ❖ **Grayscale:** This color style uses shades of gray, ranging from pure white to pure black, to portray pictures. The emphasis is on brightness levels rather than colors. For black-and-white photography, graphics, and certain printing applications where color is neither necessary nor desired, grayscale is often utilized.

To produce precise and dependable outcomes in your design tasks, it is crucial to comprehend the distinctions between and uses for each color mode. Grayscale is utilized for black and white images, whereas RGB is ideal for digital media and CMYK for print. You can guarantee that your designs will look as intended on displays and in print by choosing the right color mode.

To get the required visual effect, keep in mind how your project will look after it is finished, and pick the color mode that best suits your unique needs.

Examining The Relationship Between Bit Depth And Image Quality

Bit depth is the measure of how many bits are utilized to represent the color information in a picture. It establishes the spectrum of colors that may be seen or saved in an image file. It is possible to correctly represent more colors and shades of gray with a greater bit depth, which improves the clarity of images and the smoothness of color transitions. Bit depths of 8-bit, 16-bit, and 32-bit are the most used in Photoshop.

❖ **8-Bit:** Most digital photographs are produced with an 8-bit color depth as the default setting. Each color channel (red, green, and blue) has 256 levels of intensity available. More than 16 million different hues are now available as a result. For most design tasks where color accuracy is necessary but extreme precision is not needed, 8-bit is excellent for online graphics, digital photography, and design.

❖ **16-Bit:** When compared to 8-bit, 16-bit color depth provides a far broader variety of colors. With over 280 trillion potential colors, it offers 65,536 different degrees of intensity for each color channel. Projects requiring precise color reproduction and smooth gradients are best suited for this greater bit depth, such as professional photography, digital art, and photography. As a result, the possibility of banding or posterization is reduced and features may be preserved better.

- ❖ **32-bit:** High-dynamic-range (HDR) photographs are often created using the 32-bit color depth, sometimes referred to as floating-point. With fine brightness and exposure controls, it delivers a wide color range. The whole dynamic range of a picture must be captured and preserved in 32-bit applications such as sophisticated photo processing, visual effects, and scientific imaging.

Converting between color modes and managing color profiles

RGB, CMYK, and Grayscale are just a few of the several color options that you may deal with in Photoshop. The functions and uses of each color mode vary. However, there may be times when you need to change an image's color mode or make sure that the colors are correctly shown on all relevant screens and other outputs. It becomes essential to manage color profiles at this point.

- ❖ **Converting Color Modes:** In Photoshop, go to the picture menu, click Mode, and then pick the required color mode to convert the color mode of the picture. For instance, you may change a CMYK picture to an RGB image for online usage or vice versa for printing.

It's crucial to keep in mind that switching between color modes may cause some color shifts or loss of color information, thus it's advised to create a backup of your original picture before performing any conversions.

- ❖ **Color Profiles:** For consistent and accurate color reproduction across various devices, including monitors, printers, and other digital platforms, color profiles are crucial. As a result, hardware and software can interpret and display colors reliably. They also define the color space and properties of a device. You may assign, transform, or integrate color profiles in Photoshop to guarantee proper color representation.

- ❖ **Settings for color management:** The Color Settings menu can be found under the Edit menu and is where Photoshop's color profiles are managed. Choosing your favorite workspaces, setting default profiles, and defining how Photoshop handles color conversions and warnings are all possible here. To get precise and consistent results in your workflow for altering images, it's critical to set up color management effectively.

Your photographs will be shown and reproduced precisely across a range of devices and media if you know how to switch between color modes and maintain color profiles in Photoshop. This is especially necessary for expert printing, web design, and other visual applications where color accuracy is essential.

P.S.: For more accurate color representation during editing, it's advised to calibrate your

display on a regular basis using hardware
calibration tools.

Chapter 3

Common Image File Formats and Their Specifications

The proper file format must be chosen when dealing with digital photographs depending on your intended usage and the particular capabilities you want. Here are the four most widely used picture file formats and their main characteristics:

- ❖ **JPEG (Joint Photographic Experts Group):** Due to their effective compression method, JPEG (Joint Photographic Experts Group) is often used for pictures and online images. While keeping a high degree of picture quality, it decreases file size. JPEG is perfect for pictures with intricate features, such as portraits, and supports millions of colors. However, the compression mechanism used by JPEG might cause picture quality degradation when editing and saving JPEG photos repeatedly.

❖ **PNG (Portable Network Graphics)** is a flexible file format that is appropriate for online graphics, logos, and transparent pictures. Because it allows lossless compression, the picture quality is maintained without losing detail. PNG pictures are ideal for overlaying on various backgrounds or site designs since they may have translucent backgrounds. However, compared to JPEG, PNG files sometimes have greater file sizes, which may slow down web page loading times.

- ❖ **TIFF (Tagged Image File Format)** is a high-quality, lossless file format that is often used in graphic design and professional photography. It supports a range of bit levels, color schemes, and compression techniques. TIFF is appropriate for photos that demand the highest level of post-processing quality and flexibility. TIFF files may be fairly huge, however, which makes them less ideal for usage on the web.

- ❖ **GIF (Graphics Interchange Format):** Simple animations, pictures, and logos with few colors are often created in GIF (pictures Interchange Format). Transparency and multiple-frame animation are supported. GIF files are appropriate for usage on the web because of their modest file sizes and widespread acceptance. GIF, however, may not be appropriate for complicated graphics or photos with intricate color gradients because of its restricted color capabilities (256 colors).

The best file format should be chosen based on the intended application, the complexity of the picture, the need for transparency, and file size concerns. You may save and share your photographs with confidence if you are aware of the benefits and restrictions of each format.

Choosing the appropriate file format for web, print, and other mediums

When creating photos for diverse media, such as the web, print, or other particular applications, choosing the appropriate file format is essential. You may follow the advice in the following list to choose wisely:

Consider the following formats for photos that will be used on the web:

- ❖ **JPEG (Joint Photographic Experts Group)** is the format of choice for photos and intricate visuals with a wide range of colors. Image quality and file size reduction are well-balanced.

- ❖ **PNG (Portable Network Graphics):** For transparent pictures or straightforward graphics, use PNG (Portable Network Graphics). For logos, icons, and pictures that need transparency, PNG is often used since it provides lossless compression.

- ❖ **GIF (Graphics Interchange Format):** For straightforward animations, graphics, and pictures with few colors, GIF (Graphics Interchange Format) is the best format. Small-sized web components may be used with GIF since it provides motion and transparency.

High resolution and color fidelity should be given first priority when printing photos. It is typical to use the following formats:

- ❖ **TIFF (Tagged picture File Format:** Recommended for print applications that need the highest possible picture quality and post-processing flexibility is TIFF (Tagged picture File Format). Lossless compression is supported by TIFF, which may maintain fine detail.

❖ **Encapsulated PostScript, or EPS,** is a format that can be scaled without sacrificing quality and is ideal for vector drawings, illustrations, and print designs. With different design programs and print processes, EPS files are interoperable.

Various Media

When selecting a file format, take the unique specifications of the media into account. A few instances are:

❖ **Portable Document Format (PDF):** It is best to use the portable document format (PDF) for papers that must be shared and read uniformly across a variety of platforms and devices. In addition to text and vector graphics, PDF files may also include pictures.

❖ SVG (Scalable Vector Graphics) is an excellent choice for online graphics and drawings that need to be scalable and interactive. The editing of SVG files using vector graphic software is simple and resolution-independent.

When deciding on a format, keep in mind to balance file size, compatibility, and picture quality. It's advised to make a backup copy of your photographs in their original high-resolution form and to save a copy in the format required by the desired media.

Balancing file size and image quality

Finding the ideal ratio between file size and picture quality is crucial when dealing with digital photos. A smaller file size provides effective storage, quicker loading times, and less bandwidth utilization. Nevertheless, preserving picture quality is essential to keep the colors, details, and overall aesthetic appeal. Consider the following suggestions to assist you in finding the perfect balance:

Compression strategies

- ❖ **Lossy compression:** This technique reduces file size by discarding certain picture data. It is often used in JPEG format. By adjusting the compression level, you may strike a compromise between acceptable quality loss and file size.
- ❖ **Lossless compression:** This method reduces the file size without compromising the quality of the images. Examples of formats with lossless compression are PNG and GIF.

However, compared to lossy formats, they could produce greater file sizes.

Image Resolution:

- ❖ Analyze the needed resolution for the media you are using. Think about the display size and usual screen resolutions while using the web. Choose the appropriate print resolution (often 300 DPI) and output size. File size may be greatly decreased by resizing the picture to fit the necessary proportions.

Format choice:

- ❖ The capabilities and compression techniques used by various file formats differ. Try out several formats to see which one best meets your demands in terms of file size and picture quality.

❖ Use more recent formats like WebP or HEIC, which provide improved compression effectiveness without compromising picture quality. But make sure it works with the platform or gadget you want to use.

Use tools for compression

❖ Use internet compression tools or picture editing applications to reduce file size while maintaining image quality. These programs often include choices to change compression settings, resize photographs, or get rid of extra information.

P.S.:Keep in mind that the ideal compromise between file size and picture quality relies on your project's particular needs as well as the display medium. Make sure your photographs are optimal for both size and quality by often assessing and testing various settings and formats.

Saving and exporting images in different formats in Photoshop

Depending on your intended usage, Photoshop gives you the freedom to store and export your photos in a variety of formats. The procedures for exporting and saving photographs in various formats are as follows:

Keeping a Photo:

- ❖ Choose "Save" from the "File" menu, o r on a Mac, press Command+S or Ctrl+S.
- ❖ Select the desired folder, then type the file name.

❖ From the file format dropdown menu, choose the appropriate format (JPEG, PNG, TIFF, etc.).

❖ If necessary, configure other settings like quality, compression, and color profile.

❖ To save the picture with the selected options, click "Save".

Exporting a Photo

❖ Use the "File" menu's "Export" > "Export As" option or the Windows or Mac keyboard shortcuts Alt+Shift+Ctrl+S or Option+Shift+Command+S to export files.

❖ Select the desired folder, then type the file name.

❖ From the file format dropdown menu, choose the required format.

- ❖ If necessary, set up more choices like quality, compression, transparency, and color profile.
- ❖ To export the picture with the selected parameters, click "Export".

Popular Formats and Their Elements

- ❖ JPEG (Joint Photographic Experts Group): Excellent for photos and the web. allows for customizable compression settings, which reduces file sizes but results in some picture quality loss.
- ❖ PNG (Portable Network Graphics): Perfect for transparent pictures or when maintaining image quality is important. supports lossless compression and offers visuals of excellent quality.
- ❖ TIFF (Tagged Image File Format): This file type is often used in publishing and printing operations. provides lossless

compression while maintaining picture quality and supporting transparency and layering.

❖ Simple visuals, animations, and transparency work well with the GIF (visuals Interchange Format). uses lossless compression but can only handle 256 colors at once.

❖ When selecting the best format for storing or exporting your photographs from Photoshop, keep in mind to take into account the intended usage, quality standards, and compatibility with the destination platform or device.

Conclusion

In conclusion, "Photoshop for Beginners (Book 3): A step-by-step guide to understanding image basics in Photoshop " has guided you through the complexities of picture editing in a revolutionary way. We've looked at the fundamental ideas behind image resolution and size to help you understand how they affect the effectiveness and usability of your digital works. In order to bring your drawings to life with accuracy and vibrancy, we've also gone into the world of color modes and bit depth, unlocking the potential of RGB, CMYK, and grayscale.

Additionally, we have demystified the world of file formats by assisting you in selecting the best format for various uses, like web publishing, print, or social media sharing. You gain the ability to maximize image quality while reducing file size by being aware of the advantages and disadvantages of different file formats.

You are now prepared to confidently negotiate the complicated environment of image resolution, color modes, and file formats thanks to your newly acquired expertise. Whether you're a photographer, graphic designer, or digital artist, you have the ability to produce powerful pictures that engage your audience.

Keep in mind that practice makes perfect. Continue experimenting, improving your abilities, and discovering all the possibilities Photoshop has to offer. Expand your toolbox of skills and keep pushing the limits of your inventiveness. You'll develop more knowledge and self-assurance with each new endeavor, advancing you to even greater artistic accomplishments.

You have successfully finished reading "Photoshop for Beginners (Book 3): A step-by-step guide to understanding image basics in Photoshop." You've only just started using Photoshop, and we can't wait to see what amazing works of art and creations you come up with next. Continue learning, exploring, and letting your creativity run wild.